"HEARTLAND"
Design Book # 5

SCROLL SAW
FRETWORK PATTERNS
"Fine Line Design"™

by

Judy Gale Roberts and *Jerry Booher*

Fretwork: an ornamental design consisting of repeated and often symmetrical figures, open in relief, sometimes contained within a band or border.

Contents Design Book #5

Helpful Hints

Listed below are suggestions and helpful ideas that can be used for the projects in this book. Feel free to use whatever materials, sizes, and technique that best suit your needs.

Material list:
1/8 to 1/4" plywood, or any wood of your choosing for the fretwork cut outs.
Use a solid wood of your choosing for the shelf (mahogany, oak, etc.). Shelf material should be from 1/2" to 9/16" thickness.

Method of laying out:
Several methods for the lay out can be used;
Using a photo copier to make copies of the original drawing, use a repositioning adhesive spray applied to the back of the paper and apply the paper pattern to the face of the wood.
Using carbon paper you can carefully re-draw the pattern to transfer the layout lines onto the wood.
Using either method above carefully make a master template made of thin plywood, card board or plastic. Use this template as a master and carefully draw around it, transferring the design to the plywood or material that you are using.

CUT OUT areas marked with the x's:
CIRCLES can be drilled only, (just find a drill that most closely matches the diameter of the circle).

ADDITIONAL HINTS:
Depending on material thickness, use double sided tape or staples, stack cut at least two pieces at one time. Cutting four at one time is also feasible.
When your project is complete and assembled, try taping or gluing a colorful fabric to the backside of the fretwork pieces. This can be a solid material or have some sort of pattern on it (perhaps a material that matches your curtains or one to match your table cloth, if it is to be used in the kitchen or dinning room). This really adds to the overall effect of the design.
A wood burner may be used to add extra detail, these areas are indicated with a dashed line and are noted on the patterns which call for extra detail .
Many of the patterns indicate an area that a shelf can be placed, however, this is optional. All of these designs make nice wall hangings.

NOTE: The single black lines on this design (and many others in this book) are a single blade width cut. The saw blade kerf creates the line work which defines that portion of the fretwork. These areas could be burned if desired.

This design could be used in a number of ways. You could add "Welcome" as illustrated to the right, or extend the lower portion to add a shelf or make a key rack. This design would also look nice enlarged (to whatever size fits the maximum throat size of your saw). Also, it could easily be converted to a clock pattern, as shown to the left, by enlarging the diameter of the circle enough to add numbers.

WELCOME

Covered
Bridge

2 DB 5

This design could be used to make a key rack by extending the lower portion. If you are using 1/8" thick material you will need to add a piece of wood (as shown in the illustration to the right) to help support the hooks. The dashed lines on the pattern indicate areas that can be burned using a wood burner for extra detail.

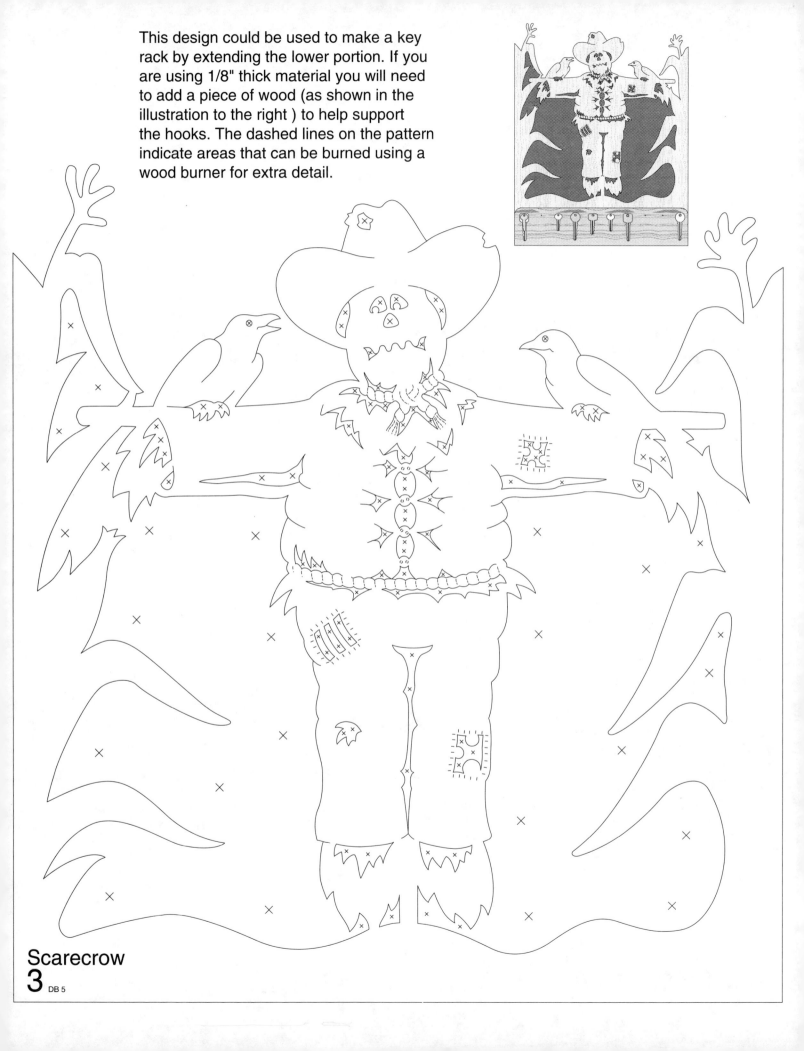

Scarecrow

3
DB 5

This pattern matches the hoe, on the following page. Put the two together, as shown below, and glue onto a contrasting background which can be placed in a frame.

Pitch Fork

This pattern matches the pitch fork on the preceding page. Put the two together, as shown below, and glue onto a contrasting background which can be placed in a frame.

Hoe

5 DB 5

This pattern can be converted
to a "free-form", as shown above,
or cut out as the pattern indicates.
This project can be put in a frame
with a contrasting background, or
it would look fine without a frame.

Check diameter for
proper size hole for
clock insert. This is a
2 3/8" diameter for a
2 13/16" clock insert.

This pattern would make a good mat for a frame (8"x10")- place your favorite photo or print behind the fretwork. A mirror could also be placed behind the fretwork.

Place photo or print here

Mail Box Mat

You may want to add a clock as indicated on the pattern, adjust the material thickness and diameter of the hole to the specifications listed for whatever clock insert you use.

Check diameter for proper size hole for clock insert. This is a 1 3/8" diameter for a 1 7/16" mini clock insert.

This design, as with others, can be made into a shelf by extending the lower portion, as shown to the left.

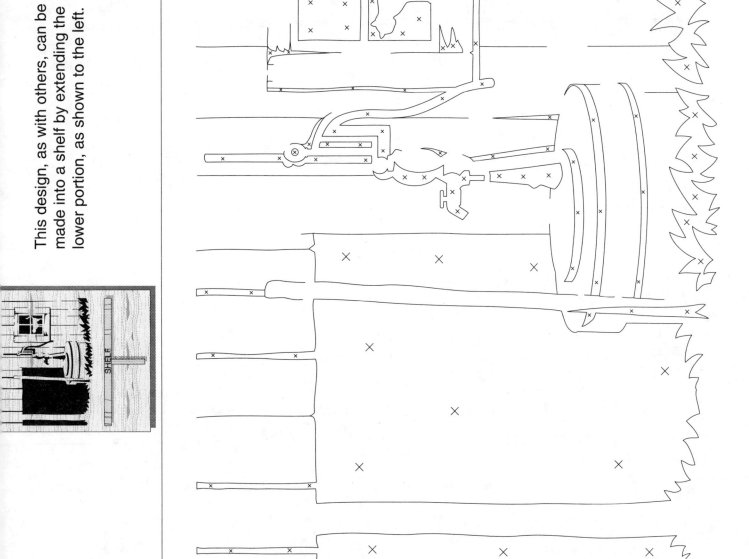

SHELF

Water Well
and Cat

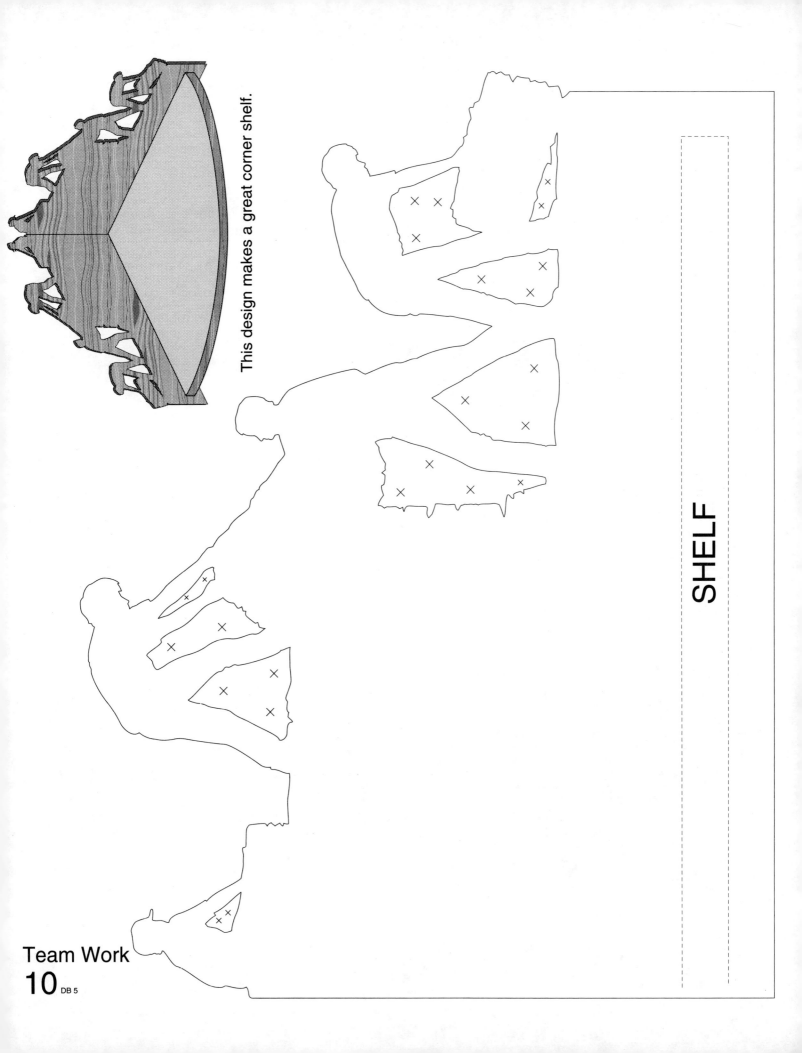

This design makes a great corner shelf.

SHELF

Team Work

The dashed lines indicate
areas to add extra detail
(on the corn leaves), use
the dashed lines as a guide
to follow with a wood burner.

WELCOME

For a 2 3/4" clock insert
cut a 2 5/16" circle (rear
mounting diameter). If adding a clock use at least
1/2" thickness of wood.

WELCOME

Welcome House
11

Use a contrasting piece of wood, paint, or fabric to place behind the fretwork to make all of the inside cuts stand out.

Farm
Country

12 DB 5

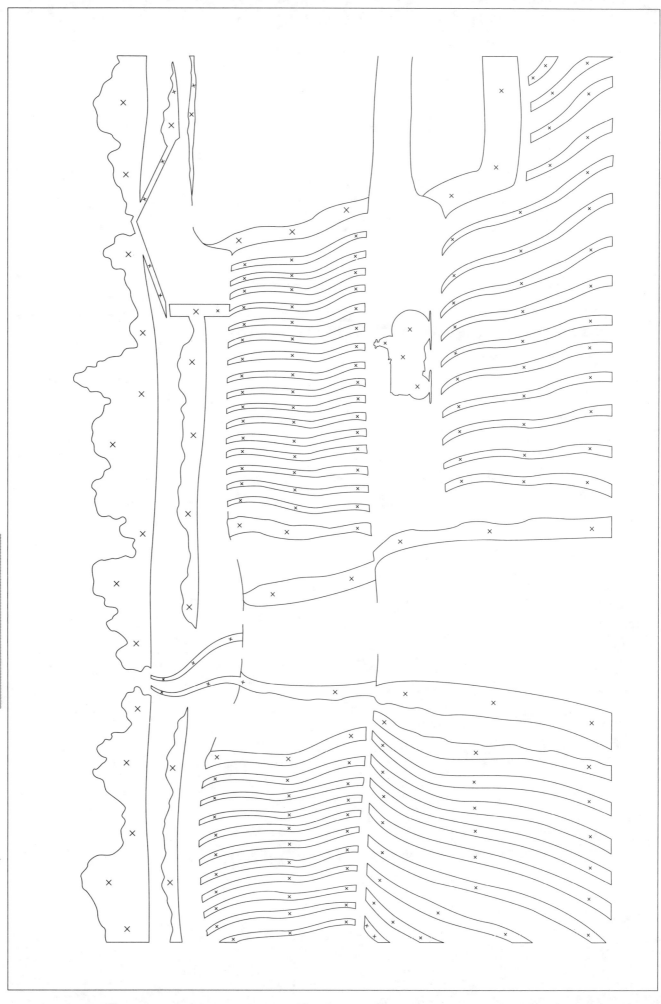

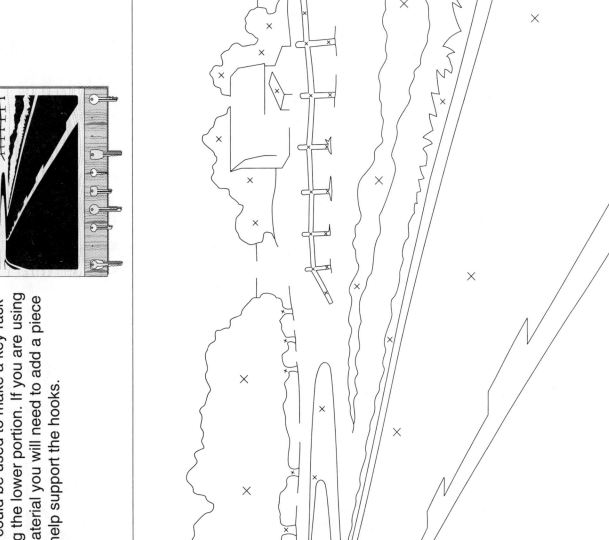

This design could be used to make a key rack by extending the lower portion. If you are using 1/8" thick material you will need to add a piece of wood to help support the hooks.

Country
Road
13 DB 5

This project would make a nice shelf by extending the lower portion, as shown to the left, or place it in a frame as shown to the right.

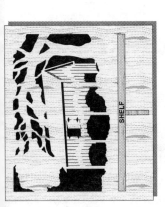

SHELF

Old Barn

14 DB 5

Field Barn

15 DB 5

Add a shelf, or just frame it.

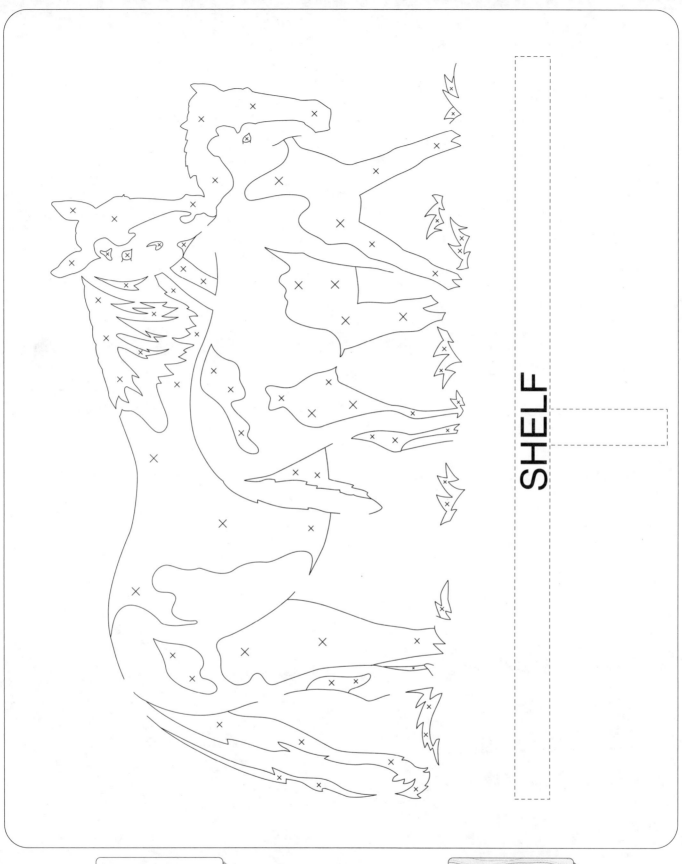

SHELF

This design would
look good with a
clock, maybe put
in a few clouds, so
the clock takes the
place of the sun
(as shown below).

Mare & Colt

16 DB 5

Cow Close Up

For added detail use a wood-burner to put the lines on the ropes, useing the dashed lines as a guide.

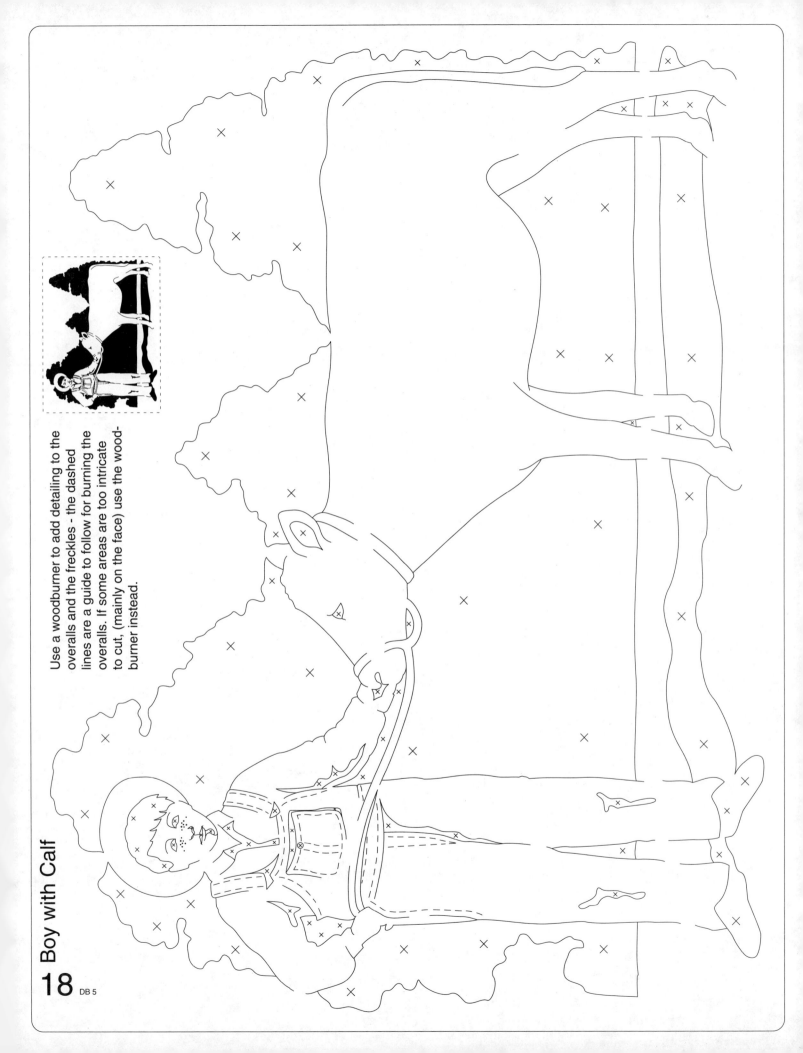

Boy with Calf

Use a woodburner to add detailing to the overalls and the freckles - the dashed lines are a guide to follow for burning the overalls. If some areas are too intricate to cut, (mainly on the face) use the woodburner instead.

18 DB 5

Napkin or Letter Holder Base

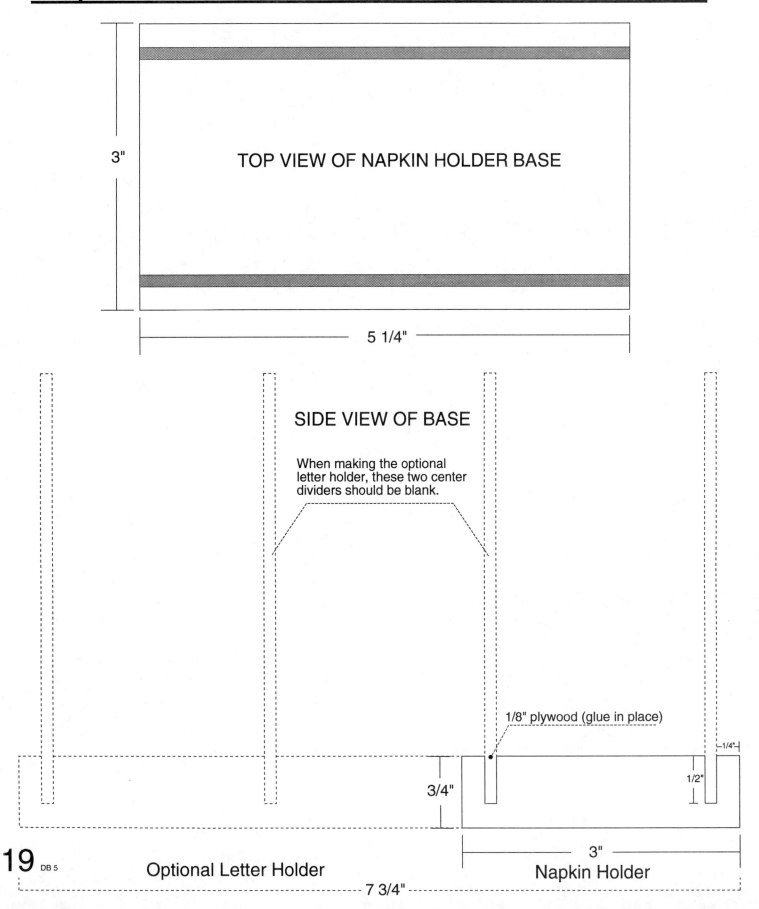

TOP VIEW OF NAPKIN HOLDER BASE

3"

5 1/4"

SIDE VIEW OF BASE

When making the optional
letter holder, these two center
dividers should be blank.

1/8" plywood (glue in place)

3/4"

1/4"

1/2"

3"

Optional Letter Holder

Napkin Holder

7 3/4"

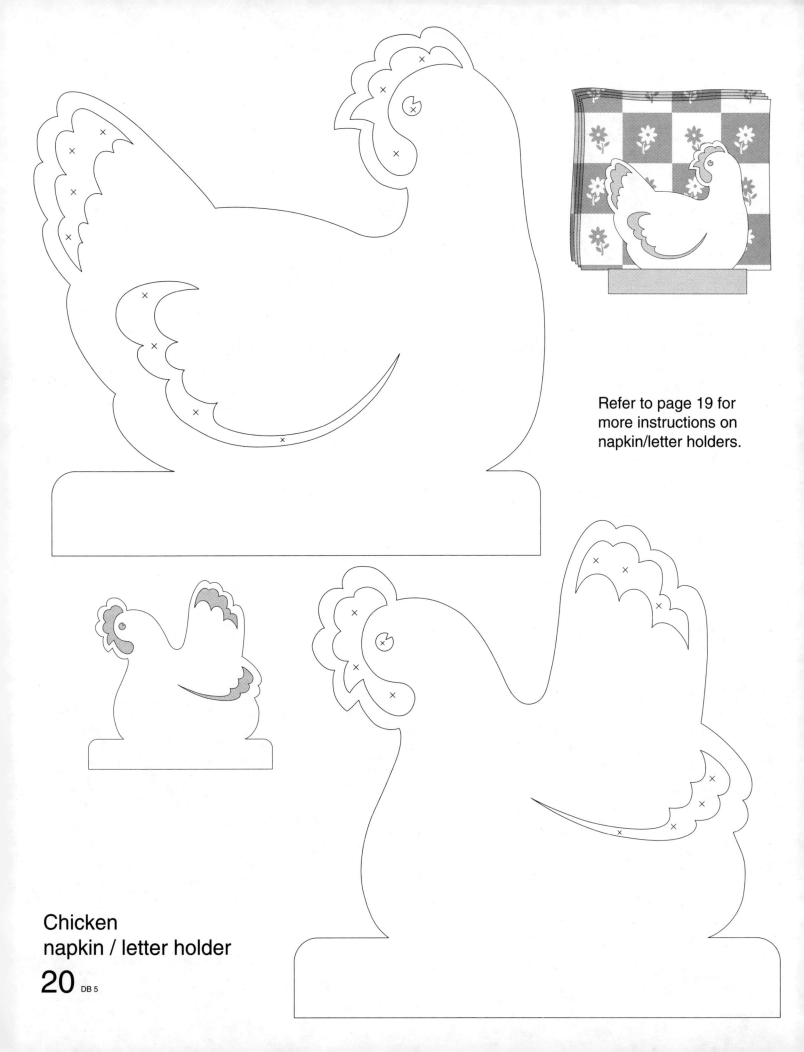

Refer to page 19 for more instructions on napkin/letter holders.

Chicken
napkin / letter holder

Refer to page 19 for more instructions on napkin/letter holders.

Chicken • Chicken Little
napkin / letter holder

21 DB 5

Refer to page 19 for more instructions on napkin/letter holders.

These napkin holders are designed to use two colors of wood, one of which could be stained or painted dark for the background (with the heart cut outs) and a light piece for the animals. After the parts are cut out, gule the light animal on top of the dark cut out (as shown in the illustrations).

Chicken • Rabbit
napkin / letter holder

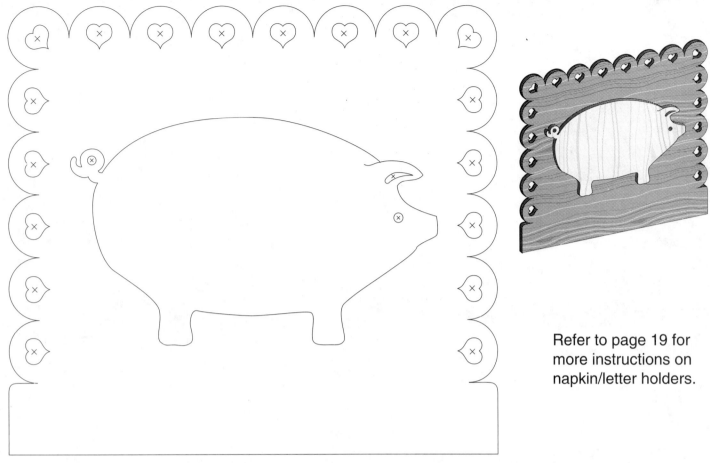

Refer to page 19 for more instructions on napkin/letter holders.

These napkin holders are designed to use two colors of wood, one of which could be stained or painted dark for the background (with the heart cut outs) and a light piece for the animals. After the parts are cut out, gule the light animal on top of the dark cut out (as shown in the illustrations).

Pig • Cow
napkin / letter holder

23 DB 5

This design makes a great wall hanging, enlarge the outer diameter (as shown above) to make a background for a clock, or extend the lower portion to add a shelf (as shown below).

SHELF

Rooster

24 DB 5

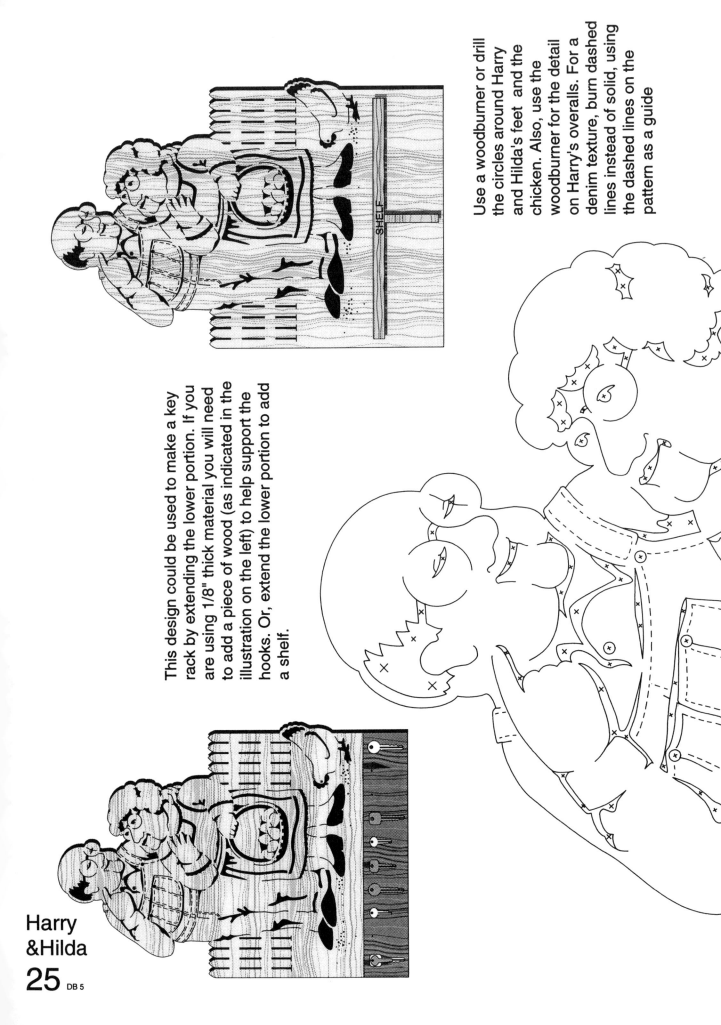

Use a woodburner or drill the circles around Harry and Hilda's feet and the chicken. Also, use the woodburner for the detail on Harry's overalls. For a denim texture, burn dashed lines instead of solid, using the dashed lines on the pattern as a guide

This design could be used to make a key rack by extending the lower portion. If you are using 1/8" thick material you will need to add a piece of wood (as indicated in the illustration on the left) to help support the hooks. Or, extend the lower portion to add a shelf.

SHELF

Harry
&Hilda

25 DB 5

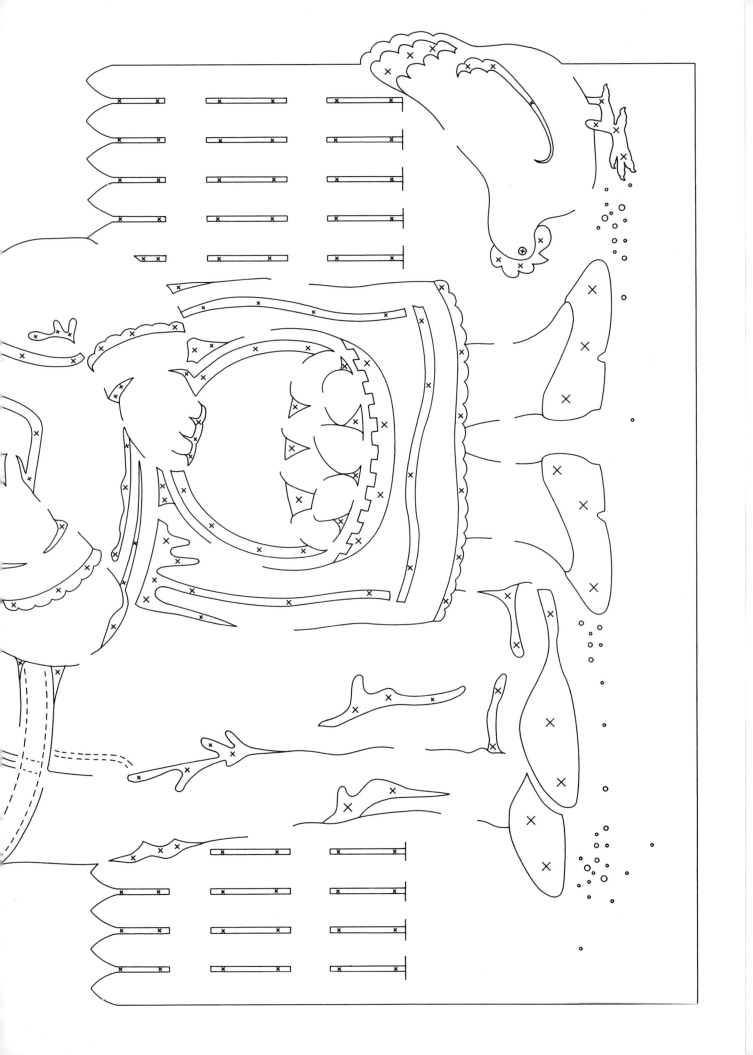

This design could easily be modified to add a clock (as shown above), I suggest using at least 1/2" thickness of wood for the project. If there is a special name you would like to add there is a place above the horse's head. This design could also be made into a shelf by extending the lower portion to accommodate a shelf and a gusset or two.

Horse & Bridle

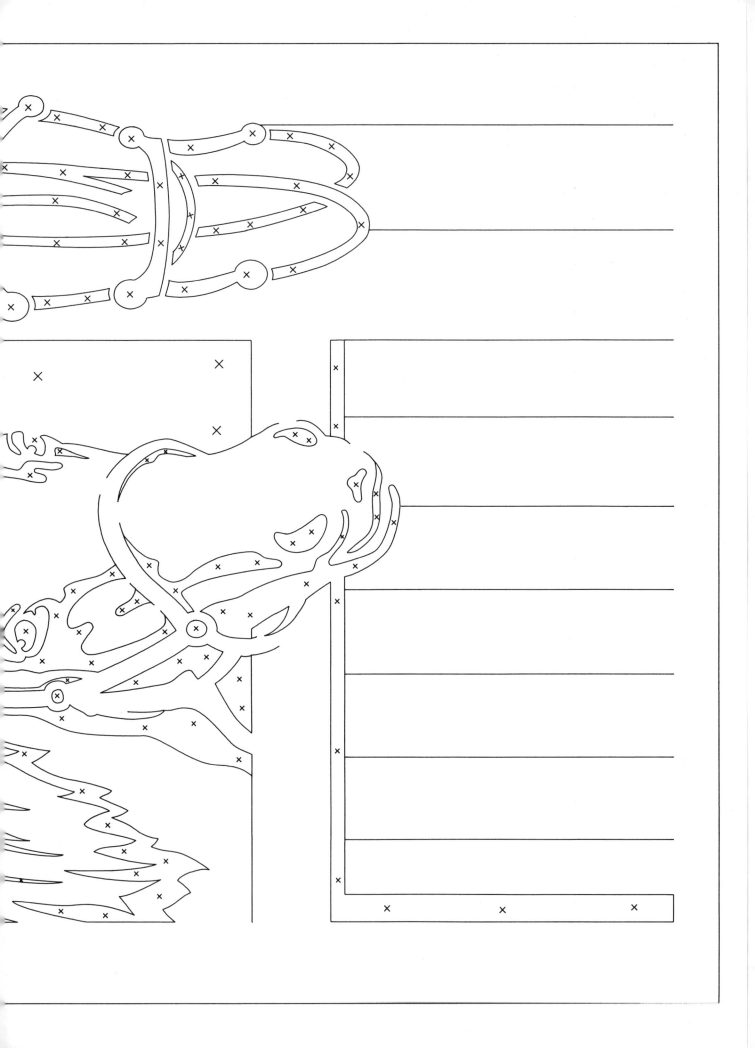

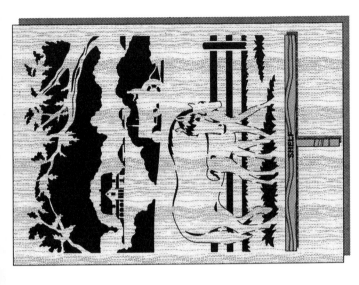

This design would look good with a contrasting color placed behind the fretwork to make all of the inside cuts stand out, and placed in a frame, or add a shelf as shown to the right.

Farm Scene

27

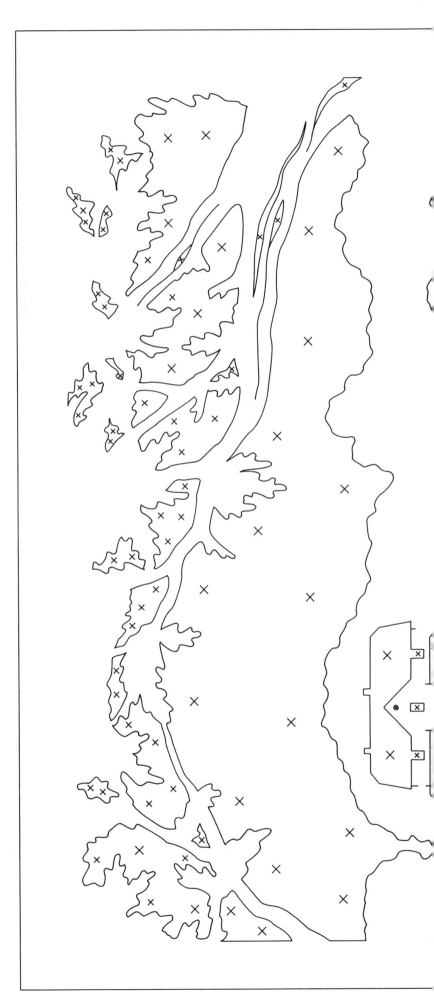

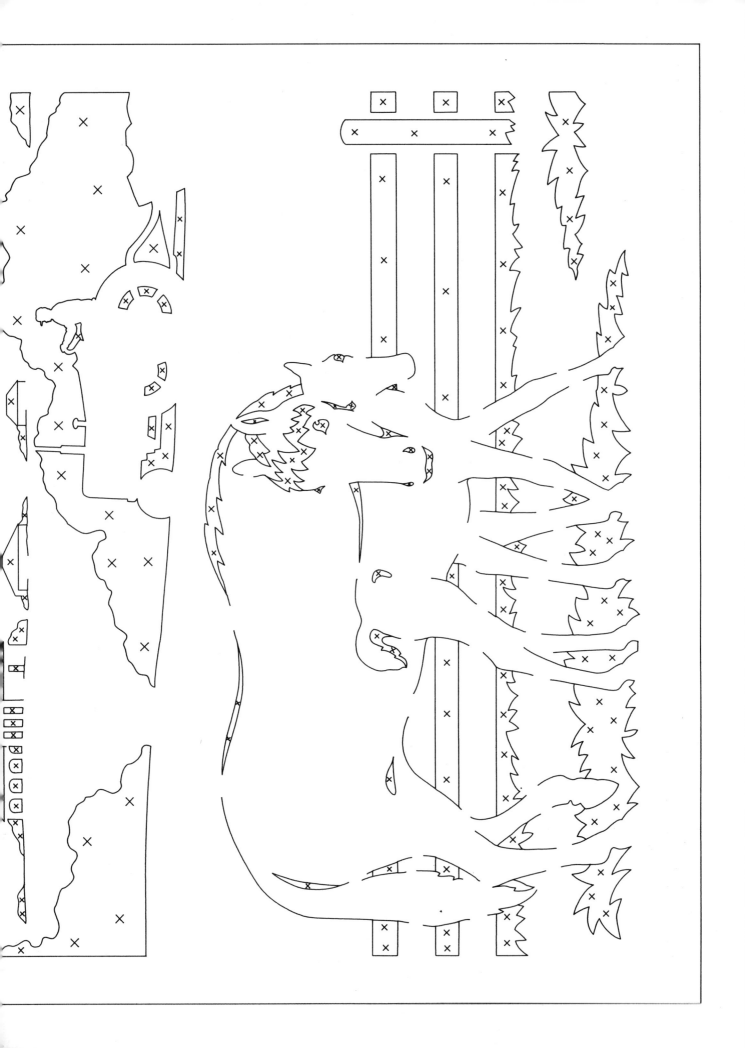

Use the patterns on the far right to cut the nose parts for the cow and the pig. Glue the noses to the areas indicated by dashed lines, as illustrated on the left.

This project would make an excellant mug rack. If you use 1/8" plywood for the fretwork portion, add at least a 1/2" thickness of wood along the lower section (indicated by dashed lines). Use pegs or hooks to hold the mugs.

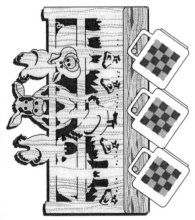

Use a woodburner or a very small drill for the circles around the chickens.

Barnyard Friends

This project was designed to go in front of the cow background on the following page. Cut both projects out and glue the cow background behind the swing pattern. If using the same color of wood for both sections, try changing the grain direction (maybe have the background horizontal and the swing portion vertical).
Other options include placing a photo of a country scene behind the fretwork, or extend the lower portion to add a shelf.

Use the dashed lines as a guide to position the cow background.

For added detail use a wood burner to burn the slats on the porch, use the dashed lines for a guide.

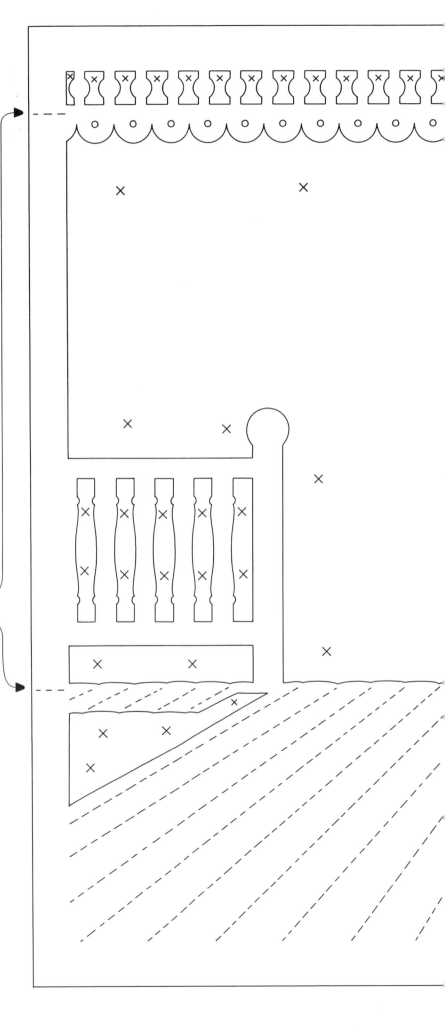

Front Porch Swing

29 DB 5

This project was designed to go behind the porch swing pattern on the previous page, as shown above. Cut both projects out and glue the cow background behind the swing pattern (the position is indicated on the porch swing pattern). If using the same color of wood for both sections, try changing the grain direction (maybe have the background horizontal and the swing portion vertical).

Other options include adding a clock, as shown below or adding a shelf as indicated on the pattern.

Cow Barn Background

SHELF

GUSSET

This design would look good with a contrasting color placed behind the fretwork to make all of the inside cuts stand out, and placed in a frame, or add a shelf as shown above.

For added detail use a wood burner to burn the lines on the front of the house, use the dashed lines for a guide.

Ol' Blue's House

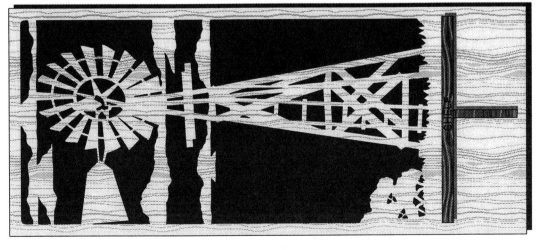

Windmill

This design would look good with a contrasting color placed behind

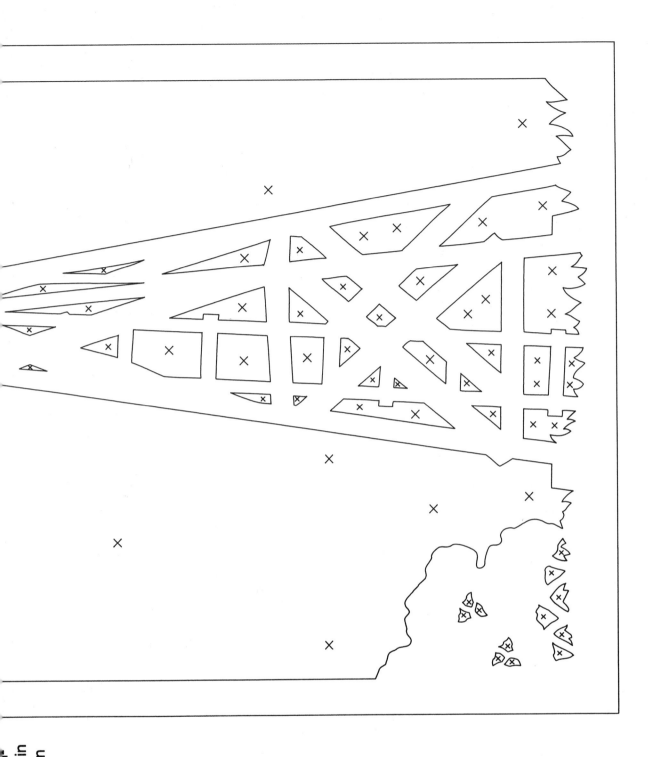

the network to make all of the line side cuts stand out, and placed in a frame, or add a shelf as shown above.

You may want to add a clock as indicated on the pattern, adjust the material thickness and diameter of the hole to the specifications listed for whatever clock insert you use.

Check diameter for proper size hole for clock insert. This is a 1 3/8" diameter for a 1 7/16" mini

Windmill & House

clock insert.

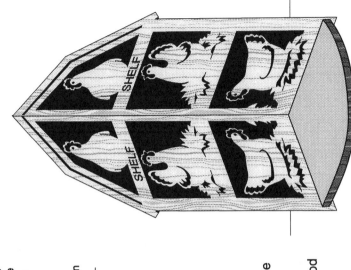

To make a corner shelf you will need to cut two halves, as shown in the illustration on the right.

Remove feet to have an optional second shelf.

Extend the side approx. 1/8" to 1/4" on both parts or just one.

Extend lower portion for a shelf.

...or make a corner shelf, using either the left half (as shown) or the right half, the dashed line on the pattern is the center line. You can stack two pieces of plywood to cut at one time.

This design has a number of possibilities, extend the lower section to add a shelf, as shown below...

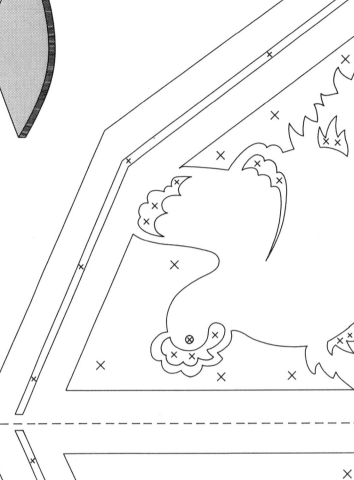

Hen House

This project was designed to use two colors of wood, dark for the background pieces (with the heart cut outs) and a light piece for the animals. After the parts are cut out, glue the light animal on top of the dark cut out, as shown in the illustration above. After the four sections are cut and glued, apply them to a solid backing (dark wood, or even a piece of fabric that matches the colors in your home) which can then be framed as shown in the illustration below.

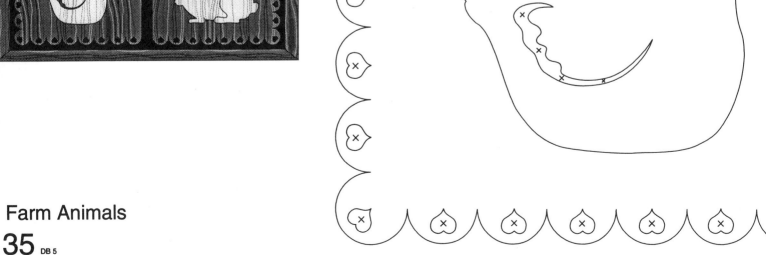

Farm Animals